W9-CJQ-362

Table of Contents

Holiday Cheese Tree

Ingredients

- 1 package (8 ounces) cream cheese, softened
- 2 cups (8 ounces) shredded Cheddar cheese
- 3 tablespoons finely chopped red bell pepper
- 3 tablespoons finely chopped onion
- 1 tablespoon lemon juice
- 2 teaspoons Worcestershire sauce
- ¾ cup chopped fresh parsley
- Yellow bell pepper
- Baby cherry tomatoes
- Lemon peel

1. Combine cheeses, chopped red bell pepper, onion, lemon juice and Worcestershire sauce in medium bowl; mix until well blended. Place on plate. Shape to form cone shape, about 6 inches tall.

2. Press parsley evenly onto cheese tree.

3. Using cookie cutter or sharp knife, cut yellow bell pepper into star. Secure star, tomatoes and lemon peel onto tree with toothpicks.

4. Serve with assorted crackers and breadsticks.

Makes about 5 cups (14 to 16 appetizer servings)

Roasted Red Pepper and Artichoke Torte

2½ cups chopped bagels (about 3 bagels)
2 tablespoons olive oil
2 packages (8 ounces each) cream cheese, softened
1 container (15 ounces) ricotta cheese
1 can (10¾ ounces) condensed cream of celery soup, undiluted
2 eggs
2 tablespoons chopped green onion
1 tablespoon dried Italian seasoning
1 clove garlic, minced
1 can (8½ ounces) artichoke hearts, drained and chopped
1 jar (15 ounces) roasted red bell peppers, drained, chopped and divided
1 cup chopped fresh basil, divided

1. Preheat oven to 375°F. Combine bagels and oil in medium bowl; mix well. Spray 9×2½-inch springform baking pan with nonstick cooking spray. Press bagel mixture into bottom and up side of prepared pan. Bake 15 minutes; cool.

2. Beat cheeses, soup, eggs, green onion, Italian seasoning and garlic with electric mixer at medium speed until well blended. Spread half of cheese mixture over bagel crust. Top with artichokes and half each of peppers and basil. Spread remaining cheese mixture over basil; top with remaining peppers. Bake 1 hour or until center is set; cool. Refrigerate 6 to 8 hours or overnight. Run knife around edge of torte; remove side of pan. Top with remaining ½ cup basil. Slice thinly; serve with crackers.

Makes 20 servings

Herbed Blue Cheese Spread with Garlic Toasts

1⅓ cups low-fat (1%) cottage cheese
1¼ cups (5 ounces) crumbled blue, feta or goat cheese
1 large clove garlic
2 teaspoons lemon juice
2 green onions with tops, sliced (about ¼ cup)
¼ cup chopped fresh basil or oregano *or* 1 teaspoon dried
   basil or oregano leaves
2 tablespoons toasted slivered almonds*
Garlic Toasts (recipe follows)

To toast almonds, spread in single layer on baking sheet. Bake in preheated 350°F oven 8 to 10 minutes or until golden brown, stirring frequently.

1. Combine cottage cheese, blue cheese, garlic and lemon juice in food processor. Cover; process until smooth. Add green onions, basil and almonds; pulse until well blended but still chunky.

2. Spoon cheese spread into small serving bowl; cover. Refrigerate until ready to serve.

3. When ready to serve, prepare Garlic Toasts. Spread 1 tablespoon cheese spread onto each toast slice. Garnish, if desired.

Makes 16 servings

Garlic Toasts

32 (½-inch-thick) French bread slices
   Nonstick cooking spray
¼ teaspoon garlic powder
⅛ teaspoon salt

Place bread slices on nonstick baking sheet. Lightly coat both sides of bread slices with cooking spray. Combine garlic powder and salt in small bowl; sprinkle evenly onto bread slices. Broil 6 to 8 inches from heat 30 to 45 seconds on each side or until bread slices are lightly toasted on both sides.

Makes 32 pieces

Herbed Blue Cheese Spread with Garlic Toasts

Pecan Cheese Balls

1 package (8 ounces) cream cheese, softened
¼ cup finely chopped fresh parsley
2 tablespoons finely chopped fresh chives
½ teaspoon Worcestershire sauce
   Dash hot pepper sauce
¾ cup finely chopped pecans
   Assorted crackers

Combine all ingredients except pecans and crackers in medium bowl. Cover; refrigerate until firm. Form cheese mixture into ball. Roll in pecans. Store tightly wrapped in plastic wrap in refrigerator. Allow cheese ball to soften at room temperature before serving with crackers.   *Makes 1 cheese ball*

Variation: Form cheese mixture into 1½-inch balls. Roll in paprika, chopped herbs (such as parsley, watercress or basil) or chopped green olives, instead of pecans.

Gift Tip: Give Pecan Cheese Ball with an assortment of other cheeses, a wooden cheese board, a jar of imported pickles or mustard, and/or a bag of pecans.

Pecan Cheese Balls (variations)

Cheesy Christmas Trees

½ cup mayonnaise
1 tablespoon dry ranch-style salad dressing mix
1 cup shredded Cheddar cheese
¼ cup grated Parmesan cheese
12 slices firm white bread
¼ cup red bell pepper strips
¼ cup green bell pepper strips

1. Preheat broiler. Combine mayonnaise and salad dressing mix in medium bowl. Add cheeses; mix well.

2. Cut bread slices into Christmas tree shapes using large cookie cutter. Spread each tree with about 1 tablespoon mayonnaise mixture. Decorate with red and green bell pepper strips. Place on baking sheet.

3. Broil 4 inches from heat 2 to 3 minutes or until bubbling. Serve warm.   *Makes about 12 appetizers*

Mini Cocktail Meatballs

1 envelope LIPTON® RECIPE SECRETS® Onion, Onion Mushroom, Beefy Mushroom or Beefy Onion Soup Mix
1 pound ground beef
½ cup plain dry bread crumbs
¼ cup dry red wine or water
2 eggs, lightly beaten

Preheat oven to 375°F.

In medium bowl, combine all ingredients; shape into 1-inch meatballs.

In shallow baking pan, arrange meatballs and bake 18 minutes or until done. Serve, if desired, with assorted mustards or tomato sauce.   *Makes about 4 dozen meatballs*

Cheesy Christmas Trees

Holiday Shrimp Mold

4½ teaspoons unflavored gelatin

¼ cup cold water

1 can (10¾ ounces) condensed tomato soup, undiluted

1 (3-ounce) package cream cheese

1 cup mayonnaise

1 (6-ounce) bag frozen small shrimp, thawed

¾ cup finely chopped celery

2 tablespoons grated onion

¼ teaspoon salt

White pepper to taste

Bell peppers for garnish (optional)

1. Dissolve gelatin in cold water in small bowl; set aside. Grease four 1-cup holiday mold pans or one 5½-cup holiday mold pan; set aside.

2. Heat soup in medium saucepan over medium heat until hot. Add cream cheese; blend well. Add gelatin mixture, mayonnaise, shrimp, celery, onion and seasonings. Pour into prepared molds; refrigerate 30 minutes. Cover with foil and refrigerate overnight.

3. Decorate with bell peppers cut into holly leaves, if desired. Serve with assorted crackers.   *Makes 12 servings*

Smoked Salmon Appetizers

¼ cup reduced-fat or fat-free cream cheese, softened
1 tablespoon chopped fresh dill *or* 1 teaspoon dried dill weed
⅛ teaspoon ground red pepper
4 ounces thinly sliced smoked salmon or lox
24 melba toast rounds or other low-fat crackers
Fresh dill sprigs (optional)

1. Combine cream cheese, dill and pepper in small bowl; stir to blend. Spread evenly over each slice of salmon. Roll up salmon slices jelly-roll style. Place on plate; cover with plastic wrap. Chill at least 1 hour or up to 4 hours before serving.

2. Using sharp knife, cut salmon rolls crosswise into ¾-inch pieces. Place pieces, cut side down, on melba rounds. Garnish each salmon roll with dill sprig, if desired. Serve cold or at room temperature. *Makes about 2 dozen appetizers*

Crostini

¼ loaf whole wheat baguette (4 ounces)
4 plum tomatoes
1 cup (4 ounces) shredded part-skim mozzarella cheese
3 tablespoons prepared pesto sauce

1. Preheat oven to 400°F. Slice baguette into 16 very thin, diagonal slices. Slice each tomato vertically into four ¼-inch slices.

2. Place baguette slices on nonstick baking sheet. Top each with 1 tablespoon cheese, then 1 slice tomato. Bake about 8 minutes or until bread is lightly toasted and cheese is melted. Remove from oven; top each crostini with about ½ teaspoon pesto sauce. Garnish with fresh basil, if desired. Serve warm.
Makes 8 appetizer servings

Smoked Salmon Appetizers

Spinach Dip

- 1 package (10 ounces) frozen chopped spinach, thawed and squeezed dry
- 1 container (16 ounces) sour cream
- 1 cup HELLMANN'S® or BEST FOODS® Mayonnaise
- 1 package KNORR® Recipe Classics™ Vegetable Soup, Dip and Recipe Mix
- 1 can (8 ounces) water chestnuts, drained and chopped (optional)
- 3 green onions, chopped

- In medium bowl, combine all ingredients; chill at least 2 hours to blend flavors.

- Stir before serving. Serve with your favorite dippers.

Makes about 4 cups dip

Yogurt Spinach Dip: Substitute 1 container (16 ounces) plain lowfat yogurt for sour cream.

Spinach and Cheese Dip: Add 2 cups (8 ounces) shredded Swiss cheese with spinach.

Prep Time: 10 minutes
Chill Time: 2 hours

Hollyberry Fruit Dip

1 tub (8 ounces) softened cream cheese
½ cup KARO® Light Corn Syrup
2 tablespoons sugar
½ cup light sour cream
1 cup cranberries, chopped
1 tablespoon grated orange peel

1. In small bowl with wire whisk or mixer at medium speed, beat cream cheese, corn syrup and sugar until fluffy. Blend in sour cream. Fold in cranberries and orange peel.

2. Chill.

3. Serve with fresh fruit dippers or shortbread cookies.

Makes about 2¼ cups

Prep Time: 10 minutes, plus chilling

Brandied Apricot Brie

1 wheel ALOUETTE® Baby Brie®, Plain
1 cup apricot preserves
1 tablespoon freshly squeezed orange juice
2 teaspoons brandy
1 teaspoon ground cinnamon
1 loaf French bread, sliced

Microwave Directions

Combine preserves, orange juice, brandy and cinnamon in microwave-safe bowl. Cover with plastic wrap and microwave on HIGH (100% power) 1½ minutes or until sauce begins to bubble. Place ALOUETTE® Baby Brie™ in shallow dish and top with apricot sauce. Microwave, uncovered, on HIGH 30 to 90 seconds or until cheese softens. Serve with French bread.

Makes 6 to 8 servings

White Pizza Dip

1 envelope LIPTON® RECIPE SECRETS® Savory Herb with Garlic Soup Mix

1 container (16 ounces) sour cream

1 cup (8 ounces) ricotta cheese

1 cup shredded mozzarella cheese (about 4 ounces), divided

¼ cup (1 ounce) chopped pepperoni (optional)

1 loaf Italian or French bread, sliced

1. Preheat oven to 350°F. In shallow 1-quart casserole, combine soup mix, sour cream, ricotta cheese, ¾ cup mozzarella cheese and pepperoni.

2. Sprinkle with remaining ¼ cup mozzarella cheese.

3. Bake uncovered 30 minutes or until heated through. Serve with bread. *Makes 3 cups dip*

Prep Time: 10 minutes
Cook Time: 30 minutes

Cranberry-Glazed Brie

Ingredients

Cornmeal

¾ cup canned whole berry cranberry sauce, well drained

¼ teaspoon dry mustard

⅛ teaspoon ground ginger

⅛ teaspoon ground cloves

⅛ teaspoon ground allspice

1 package (17¼ ounces) frozen puff pastry sheets, thawed

1 round (15 ounces) fully ripened Brie cheese

1 egg

1 tablespoon water

Green, red and yellow food colorings

Sliced pears and/or assorted crackers

1. Preheat oven to 400°F. Lightly sprinkle baking sheet with cornmeal.

2. Combine cranberry sauce, dry mustard and spices; mix well.

3. Place 1 puff pastry sheet on lightly floured surface; roll out pastry 2 inches larger than diameter of cheese round. Place cheese in center of pastry. Cut away excess pastry, leaving 1-inch rim around bottom of cheese; reserve trimmings. Place pastry and cheese on prepared baking sheet. Spread cranberry mixture onto top of cheese to within 1 inch of edge.

4. Roll out remaining pastry sheet large enough to completely cover cheese. Place pastry over cheese; trim away excess pastry. (Be sure to leave 1-inch rim of pastry at bottom of cheese.) Cut slits in top of pastry to allow steam to escape.

5. Combine egg and water; beat lightly with fork. Brush onto pastry to cover completely. Fold up bottom rim of pastry; press edges together to seal.

6. Cut out leaf shapes or other decorative designs from pastry trimmings. Attach cutouts to top of pastry-covered cheese with remaining egg mixture; brush with food colorings that have been diluted slightly with water.

7. Bake 15 minutes. Reduce oven temperature to 350°F. Continue baking 15 to 20 minutes or until pastry is golden brown. Remove to wire rack; let stand 15 minutes before cutting to serve. Serve warm with pear slices or crackers.   *Makes 12 appetizer servings*

Egg Champignons

6 eggs, hard cooked, peeled and chopped

¼ cup dry bread crumbs

¼ cup (1 ounce) crumbled blue cheese

2 tablespoons thinly sliced green onions with tops

2 tablespoons dry white wine

2 tablespoons butter, melted

1 tablespoon chopped fresh parsley *or* 1½ teaspoons dried
    parsley flakes

½ teaspoon garlic salt

24 large mushroom caps (about 1½ inches in diameter)

    Paprika (optional)

    Green onions and tomato slices for garnish

1. Preheat oven to 450°F. Lightly grease baking sheet. Combine eggs, bread crumbs, blue cheese, 2 tablespoons green onions, wine, butter, parsley and garlic salt in medium bowl.

2. Fill each mushroom cap with 1 rounded tablespoonful egg mixture. Place mushroom caps on prepared baking sheet.

3. Bake 8 to 10 minutes. Sprinkle with paprika and garnish, if desired.   *Makes 8 first-course servings*

Elegant Shrimp Scampi

6 tablespoons butter

6 to 8 large cloves garlic, minced

1½ pounds large raw shrimp (about 16), peeled and deveined

6 green onions, thinly sliced

¼ cup dry white wine

Juice of 1 lemon (about 2 tablespoons)

¼ cup chopped fresh parsley

Salt and black pepper to taste

Lemon slices and fresh parsley sprigs for garnish (optional)

1. Clarify butter by melting it in small saucepan over low heat. *Do not stir.* Skim off white foam that forms on top. Strain clarified butter through cheesecloth into glass measuring cup to yield ⅓ cup. Discard milky residue at bottom of pan.

2. Heat clarified butter in large skillet over medium heat. Add garlic; cook and stir 1 to 2 minutes until softened but not brown.

3. Add shrimp, green onions, wine and lemon juice; cook and stir until shrimp turn pink and are firm and opaque, 1 to 2 minutes on each side.

4. Just before serving, add chopped parsley and season with salt and pepper. Serve on individual shell-shaped or small gratin dishes. Garnish, if desired.   *Makes 8 servings*

Marinated Mushrooms

1 pint whole, uniformly sized, small white button
    mushroom caps, washed

½ cup olive oil

3 tablespoons tarragon vinegar

¼ cup finely chopped fresh parsley

1 tablespoon Dijon-style mustard

3 cloves garlic, finely chopped

1 teaspoon sugar

¾ teaspoon dried tarragon leaves, crushed

½ teaspoon salt

   Black pepper

Fill 16-ounce jar with mushrooms. Process remaining ingredients in food processor or combine in small bowl with wire whisk. Pour dressing into jar to cover mushrooms completely. Seal jar and marinate overnight at room temperature to blend flavors. Store up to 1 week in refrigerator. Bring to room temperature before serving.   *Makes about 6 servings or 3 cups mushrooms*

Tip: If giving as a gift, arrange mushrooms attractively in a pretty jar.

Acknowledgments

The publisher would like to thank the companies and organizations listed below for the use of their recipes and photographs in this publication.

ACH FOOD COMPANIES, INC.

Alouette® Cheese, Chavrie® Cheese, Saladena®

Unilever Foods North America